Inessential Things
poems and pictures

Edited by Helen J Bate

In Memory of
Douglas Dutton
(1917-1998)

A very special thank you to John Killick who has
supported us for many years and has contributed
his time and expertise to assist in the selection
of the poems for this book.

**Pictures
to share**

First published in 2015 by
Pictures to Share Community Interest Company,
a UK based social enterprise that publishes
illustrated books for older people.

www.picturestoshare.co.uk

Printed in Europe

ISBN 978-0-9563818-9-7

2

Introduction

Genuine poetry can communicate before it is understood.

T. S. Eliot (1888 - 1965)

Poetry, like fairy cakes and butterflies, may be seen by some as just another one of those inessential things that have no importance in our day to day life.

On the other hand, poetry can successfully express things that otherwise would be almost impossible to put into words.

Poetry can help us to understand what life is all about; the wonder of the natural world, the pleasures, pain or disappointments of love, the humour and horror of humanity, and the joy, fear and sadness that is all part of being alive.

Poetry has an ability to tap into our innermost feelings, to make us think, laugh or cry, and to trigger distant memories.

Even when we cannot fully understand the meaning of the words, poetry can sometimes help us to rediscover emotions and feelings that lie buried deep within our soul.

Valentine

by Wendy Cope

My heart has made its mind up
And I'm afraid it's you.
Whatever you've got lined up,
My heart has made its mind up
And if you can't be signed up
This year, next year will do.
My heart has made its mind up
And I'm afraid it's you.

Inessential Things

by Brian Patten

What do cats remember of days?

They remember the ways in from the cold,
The warmest spot, the place of food.
They remember the places of pain, their enemies,
The irritation of birds, the warm fumes of the soil,
The usefulness of dust.
They remember the creak of a bed, the sound
Of their owner's footsteps,
The taste of fish, the loveliness of cream.
Cats remember what is essential of days.
Letting all other memories go as if of no worth
They sleep sounder than we,
Whose hearts break remembering
So many inessential things.

If by Rudyard Kipling

If you can keep your head when all about you
    Are losing theirs and blaming it on you,
If you can trust yourself when all men doubt you,
    But make allowance for their doubting too;
If you can wait and not be tired by waiting,
    Or being lied about, don't deal in lies,
Or being hated, don't give way to hating,
    And yet don't look too good, nor talk too wise:

If you can dream - and not make dreams your master;
    If you can think - and not make thoughts your aim;
If you can meet with Triumph and Disaster
    And treat those two impostors just the same;
If you can bear to hear the truth you've spoken
    Twisted by knaves to make a trap for fools,
Or watch the things you gave your life to, broken,
    And stoop and build 'em up with worn-out tools:

If you can talk with crowds and keep your virtue,
    Or walk with Kings - nor lose the common touch,
If neither foes nor loving friends can hurt you,
    If all men count with you, but none too much;
If you can fill the unforgiving minute
    With sixty seconds' worth of distance run -
Yours is the Earth and everything that's in it,
    And - which is more - you'll be a Man, my son!

Mother Doesn't Want a Dog

by Judith Viorst

Mother doesn't want a dog.
Mother says they smell,
And never sit when you say sit,
Or even when you yell.
And when you come home late at night
And there is ice and snow,
You have to go back out because
The dumb dog has to go.

Mother doesn't want a dog.
Mother says they shed,
And always let the strangers in
And bark at friends instead,
And do disgraceful things on rugs,
And track mud on the floor,
And flop upon your bed at night
And snore their doggy snore.

Mother doesn't want a dog.
She's making a mistake.
Because, more than a dog, I think
She will not want this snake.

First Day

by Bernard Kops

He went from us,
He ran from us
into crowds of empty space,
into face and face and face,
he took his place.

He went, he went at last.
Too soon he went,
he ran from us.

Too late he went;
he went, he went so fast.

He smiled and then he waved
for us.

We laughed and smiled
and wavered back.

He took his place and went from us.

We smiled and smiled and smiled back.

Then he was gone and lost in play;
into the playground of the pain,
away from the crying of the heart,
into the thankyou of the brain.

1502

14

Dürer's Hare

by Anna Wigley

Still trembling, after five hundred years.
Still with the smell of grass
and the blot of summer rain
on her long, thorn-tipped paws.

Look how thick the fur is,
and how each thistledown hair
catches the light
that glistens even in shadow
from the trimmed plush of the ears.

How did he keep her still?
She was crouched there long enough
for him to trace the fragile hips
and ribs beneath the mink,
to feel the pale edges
of the belly-pouch,
the sprung shutters of the flanks.
The nose shimmers
where the short hairs grow in a rosette.
Go on, touch it.

For she's only here for a moment,
Dürer's hare;
the frame can barely hold her.
Her shadow is a shifting thing,
slippery as a raincloud in wind,
and even as you look,
twitches to be gone.

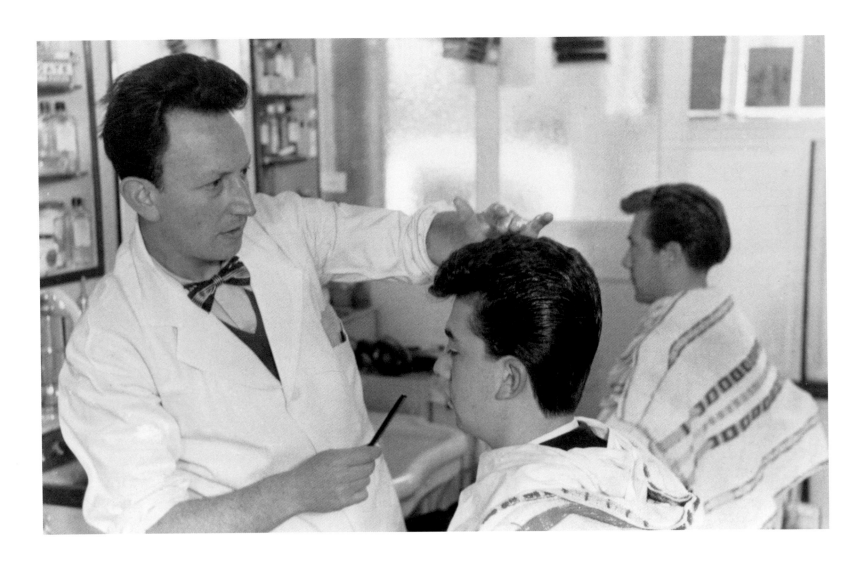

The Barber's

by Walter de la Mare

Gold locks, and black locks,
Red locks and brown,
Topknot to love-curl
The hair wisps down;
Straight above the clear eyes,
Rounded round the ears,
Snip-snap and snick-a-snick,
Clash the Barber's shears;

Us, in the looking-glass,
Footsteps in the street,
Over, under, to and fro,
The lean blades meet;
Bay Rum or Bear's Grease,
A silver groat to pay -
Then out a-shin-shan-shining
In the bright, blue day.

Can't Abear

by Walter de la Mare

I can't abear a Butcher,
I can't abide his meat,
The ugliest shop of all is his,
The ugliest in the street;
Bakers' are warm, cobblers' dark,
Chemists' burn watery lights;
But oh, the sawdust butcher's shop,
That ugliest of sights.

Love is...

by Adrian Henri

Love is feeling cold in the back of vans
Love is a fan club with only two fans
Love is walking holding paint stained hands
Love is

Love is fish and chips on winter nights
Love is blankets full of strange delights
Love is when you don't put out the light
Love is

Love is the presents in Christmas shops
Love is when you're feeling Top of the Pops
Love is what happens when the music stops
Love is

Love is white panties lying all forlorn
Love is pink nightdresses still slightly warm
Love is when you have to leave at dawn
Love is

Love is you and love is me
Love is prison and love is free
Love's what's there when you are away from me
Love is...

The door

by Miroslav Holub

Go and open the door.	Maybe outside there's
a tree, or a wood,
a garden,
or a magic city.

Go and open the door.	Maybe a dog's rummaging.
Maybe you'll see a face,
or an eye
or the picture of a picture.

Go and open the door.	If there's a fog
it will be clear.

Go and open the door.	Even if there's only
the darkness ticking,
even if there's only
the hollow wind,
even if nothing is there,

Go and open the door.	At least
there'll be
a draught...

Save the Last Dance for Me

by Doc Pomus and Mort Shuman

You can dance, every dance with the guy
Who gives you the eye, let him hold you tight.
You can smile, every smile for the man
Who held your hand 'neath the pale moonlight,

But don't forget who's taking you home,
And in whose arms you're gonna be,
So darlin', save the last dance for me.

Oh I know, Oh I know, that the music's fine
Like sparkling wine, go and have your fun.
Laugh and sing, but while we're apart
Don't give your heart to anyone,

Baby, don't you know I love you so?
Can't you feel it when we touch?
I will never, never let you go
I love you, oh, so much.

You can dance, go and carry on
Till the night is gone and it's time to go.
If he asks, if you're all alone,
Can he take you home, you must tell him, no,

'Cause don't forget who's taking you home
And in whose arms you're gonna be
So darlin', save the last dance for me.

from

The Song of Wandering Aengus

by William Butler Yeats

Though I am old with wandering
Through hollow lands and hilly lands,
I will find out where she has gone,
And kiss her lips and take her hands;

And walk among long dappled grass,
And pluck till time and times are done,
The silver apples of the moon,
The golden apples of the sun.

Daddy Fell into the Pond

by Alfred Noyes

Everyone grumbled. The sky was grey.
We had nothing to do and nothing to say.
We were nearing the end of a dismal day,
And there seemed to be nothing beyond,

THEN Daddy fell into the pond!

And everyone's face grew merry and bright,
And Timothy danced for sheer delight.
"Give me the camera, quick, oh quick!
He's crawling out of the duckweed."
   Click!

Then the gardener suddenly slapped his knee,
And doubled up, shaking silently,
And the ducks all quacked as if they were daft
And it sounded as if the old drake laughed.
Oh, there wasn't a thing that didn't respond

WHEN

Daddy fell into the pond!

from
The Raven

by Edgar Allan Poe

Once upon a midnight dreary, while I pondered, weak and weary,
Over many a quaint and curious volume of forgotten lore—
While I nodded, nearly napping, suddenly there came a tapping,
As of some one gently rapping, rapping at my chamber door.
"'Tis some visitor," I muttered, "tapping at my chamber door—
    Only this and nothing more."

And the silken, sad, uncertain rustling of each purple curtain
Thrilled me—filled me with fantastic terrors never felt before;
So that now, to still the beating of my heart, I stood repeating
"'Tis some visitor entreating entrance at my chamber door—
Some late visitor entreating entrance at my chamber door;—
    This it is and nothing more."

Presently my soul grew stronger, hesitating then no longer,
"Sir," said I, "or Madam, truly your forgiveness I implore;
But the fact is I was napping, and so gently you came rapping,
And so faintly you came tapping, tapping at my chamber door,
That I scarce was sure I heard you"—here I opened wide the door;—
    Darkness there and nothing more.

Adapted extract from

Get Drunk
by Charles Baudelair

Always be drunk.
That's it!

The great imperative!

In order not to feel
Time's horrid fardel
bruise your shoulders,
grinding you into the earth,

Get drunk and stay that way.

On what?

On wine, poetry,
virtue, whatever.

But get drunk.

And if you sometimes happen to wake up
on the porches of a palace,

in the green grass of a ditch,
in the dismal loneliness of your own room,
your drunkenness gone or disappearing,

ask the wind,
the wave,
the star,
the bird,
the clock,
ask what time it is;

and the wind,
the wave,
the star,
the bird,
the clock
will answer you:

"Time to get drunk!"

At the Circus

by Robert Nye

All one wet day we waited for it,
Entering at darkfall the big top
Pitched in a muddy field on the edge of town.

Drumming of rain on that canvas roof!
Lights!
Music!
Clowns with sad faces!
Jugglers and acrobats!
Fire!

Horses!
And lo, George Sanger's famous elephants
Trumpeting in behind their stink,
Their trunks erect, their feet so delicate
You might have thought that they were dancing...

But here's the wonder:
My little son
Who'd talked of nothing else but elephants
(because he's never seen an elephant)
Shut his bright eyes to breathe in elephant
And fell asleep with surfeit of delight
And did not wake until the show was over.

Bike with
no Hands

by Helena Nelson

One look at you and I knew
you'd be able to ride a bike with no hands.

I'd tried it, of course, but could never do it.
It was written all over your face that you
would have practised, bare legs, bloody knees,
in the Summer evenings, hours at a time
when no-one was watching the mishaps, until
casually, coolly, at infinite ease,
you'd ride, no-handed, surveying the street,
as if you'd been born on a circus bike.

I wish - but then, we are what we are.
I drive with two hands, walk with both feet
firmly planted on sensible ground. And
I've got you. Who can ride with no hands.

Love Songs in Age

by Philip Larkin

She kept her songs, they took so little space,
The covers pleased her:
One bleached from lying in a sunny place,
One marked in circles by a vase of water,
One mended, when a tidy fit had seized her,
And coloured by her daughter -
So they had waited, till in widowhood
She found them, looking for something else, and stood

Relearning how each frank submissive chord
Had ushered in
Word after sprawling, hyphenated word,
And the unfailing sense of being young
Spread out like a spring-woken tree, wherein
That hidden freshness sung,
That certainty of time laid up in store
As when she played them first. But even more

The glare of that much-mentioned brilliance, love,
Broke out, to show
Its bright incipience sailing above,
Still promising to solve, and satisfy,
And set unchangeably in order. So
To pile them back, to cry,
Was hard, without lamely admitting how
It had not done so then, and could not now.

'Hope' is the Thing with Feathers

by Emily Dickinson

'Hope' is the thing with feathers
That perches in the soul,
And sings the tune without the words,
And never stops - at all.

And sweetest in the Gale is heard;
And sore must be the storm
That could abash the little Bird
That kept so many warm.

I've heard it in the chilliest land
And on the strangest Sea;
Yet, never, in Extremity,
It asked a crumb of me.

'Sooeep!'

by Walter de la Mare

Black as a chimney is his face,
And ivory white his teeth,
And in his brass-bound cart he rides,
The chestnut blooms beneath.

'Sooeep, Sooeep!' he cries, and brightly peers
This way and that to see
With his two light-blue shining eyes
What custom there may be.

And once inside the house, he'll squat,
And drive his rods on high,
Till twirls his sudden sooty brush
Against the morning sky.

Then, 'mid his bulging bags of soot,
With half the world asleep,
His small cart wheels him off again,
Still hoarsely bawling, 'Sooeep !'

Escape at Bedtime

by R.L.Stevenson

The lights from the parlour and kitchen shone out
Through the blinds and the windows and bars;
And high overhead and all moving about,
There were thousands of millions of stars.
There ne'er were such thousands of leaves on a tree,
Nor of people in church or the Park,
As the crowds of the stars that looked down upon me,
And that glittered and winked in the dark.

The Dog, and the Plough, and the Hunter, and all,
And the star of the sailor, and Mars,
These shone in the sky, and the pail by the wall
Would be half full of water and stars.
They saw me at last, and they chased me with cries,
And they soon had me packed into bed;
But the glory kept shining and bright in my eyes,
And the stars going round in my head.

from

Caterpillar

by Norman MacCaig

He stands on the suckers under his tail,
stretches forward and puts down
his six legs. Then he brings up
the sucker under his tail, making
a beautiful loop.

That's his way of walking. He makes
a row of upside down U's
along the rib of a leaf.
He is as green as it.

He stands on his tail
on the very tip of the leaf and sways,
sways like a tiny charmed snake,
groping in empty space for a foothold
where none is, where there is no
foothold at all.

I Wandered Lonely as a Cloud

by William Wordsworth

I wandered lonely as a cloud
That floats on high o'er vales and hills,
When all at once I saw a crowd,
A host, of golden daffodils;

Beside the lake, beneath the trees,
Fluttering and dancing in the breeze.
Continuous as the stars that shine
And twinkle on the milky way,
They stretched in never-ending line
Along the margin of a bay:
Ten thousand saw I at a glance,
Tossing their heads in sprightly dance.

The waves beside them danced; but they
Out-did the sparkling waves in glee:
A poet could not but be gay,
In such a jocund company:
I gazed - and gazed - but little thought
What wealth the show to me had brought:

For oft, when on my couch I lie
In vacant or in pensive mood,
They flash upon that inward eye
Which is the bliss of solitude;
And then my heart with pleasure fills,
And dances with the daffodils.

from
Spring Rain

by Sara Teasdale

I remembered a darkened doorway
Where we stood while the storm swept by,
Thunder gripping the earth
And lightning scrawled on the sky.

The passing motor busses swayed,
For the street was a river of rain,
Lashed into little golden waves
In the lamp light's stain.

With the wild spring rain and thunder
My heart was wild and gay;
Your eyes said more to me that night
Than your lips would ever say. . . .

I thought I had forgotten,
But it all came back again
To-night with the first spring thunder
In a rush of rain.

The Beautiful Day

by Helena Nelson

On the beautiful, beautiful day
nobody moped or cried
or said that lemonade
was too expensive to buy

and the sun was not too hot
and the wind was not too strong
and the sandwiches tasted right
and the journey was not too long

and the river was bright and cold
and we paddled and splashed in fun
and were good – as good as gold –
and we shared the gold we spun

and when it was time for home
nobody seemed to mind
and the car was snug and warm
and we all sang 'Clementine'

and our darling beds were fine
with sheets fresh-ironed like dew
and we slept from dusk to dawn…
it was beautiful, and it was true.

I Still Haven't Given up Hope

by Pam Ayres

I still haven't given up hope you know,
I still await the day,
When my true romantic hero
comes to carry me away,
Well I've been married thirty years,
some people find that long,
But my husband's just a stop-gap
till the real one comes along.

Then like Lawrence of Arabia
across the burning sand,
I see him ride towards me
and I take his outstretched hand,
I see his pearly teeth,
the flash of sunlight on enamel,
And if love cannot sustain us,
we shall have to eat the camel.

Some brief information about the poets

Pam Ayres (b 1947) appeared on the TV talent show, Opportunity Knocks in 1975 and this proved to be the start of a long and successful career writing and performing poetry.

Charles Beaudelair (1821 - 1867) was a French poet who was credited with coining the term 'modernity' to define the ephemeral style of modern city life. He considered it was the responsibility of artists to portray this.

Emily Bronte (1818 - 1848) was an English novelist and poet who is best known for her only novel, Wuthering Heights,

Wendy Cope OBE (b 1945) writes poetry that is perhaps best known for its humour and wit.

Emily Dickinson (1830 - 1886) was an American poet who wrote around 1,000 poems in her 20's and 30's. These remained unpublished until after her death at 55 years of age.

Adrian Henri (1932 - 2000) came to prominence as a poet in the groundbreaking Penguin anthology The Mersey Sound (1967), one of the best-selling poetry books of all time.

Molly Holden (1927 - 1981) was confined to a wheelchair in later life. Her poems often explore the undramatic world of the countryside, the house and the garden.

Miroslav Holub (1923 - 1998) was a Czech research scientist who also wrote poetry.

Rudyard Kipling (1865 - 1936) was born in India but spent his later years in England. He is best known for his Jungle Book stories.

Bernard Kops (b 1926) is a successful dramatist, poet and novelist. The son of Dutch Jewish immigrants, he lives in London with his wife Erica.

Philip Larkin CBE (1922 - 1985) was born in Coventry and graduated in English from St John's College, Oxford. He worked as a librarian throughout his life, whilst at the same time publishing many collections of poetry.

Norman MacCaig OBE (1910 - 1996) divided his time between the West Highlands of Scotland and Edinburgh. He wrote virtually nothing but poems which cumulatively make up an impressive body of work.

Walter de la Mare (1873 - 1956) English writer and poet. His ashes are buried in St Paul's Cathedral where he was once a choir boy.

Helena Nelson writes both serious and light verse. She is also the originator and editor of HappenStance Press, an independent poetry press www.happenstancepress.org

Alfred Noyes CBE (1880 - 1958) was an English poet who aimed in many of his poems to "follow the careless and happy feet of children back into the kingdom of those dreams which...are the sole reality worth living and dying for."

Robert Nye (b 1939) is a successful English playwright, author and poet. He has been described as one of the most interesting poets writing today.

Brian Patten (b 1946) made his name in the 1960s as one of the Liverpool Poets. As well as poetry for adults he is also well-known for his best-selling poetry collections for children.

Edgar Allan Poe (1809 - 1849) was an American author and poet considered part of the American Romantic Movement and best known for his tales of mystery and the macabre.

Robert Louis Stevenson (1850 - 1894) was a Scottish novelist and poet. His most famous works are Treasure Island and the Strange Case of Dr Jekyll and Mr Hyde.

Sara Teasdale (1884 - 1933) was an American poet. She divorced in 1929 and lived the rest of her life as a semi-invalid. Teasdale committed suicide at the age of 48.

Judith Viorst (b 1931) is an American author of psychology books, children's books and poetry.

Anna Wigley (b 1962) was born and lives in Cardiff. She has been described as one of Wales' most sensitive lyric poets,

William Wordsworth (1770 - 1850) was a major English Romantic poet.

William Butler Yeats (1865 - 1939) is widely considered to be one of the greatest poets of the twentieth century. He was proud of his Irish heritage and many of his poems are based on Irish legends, folklore, ballads and songs.

Poem and Picture credits

**Pictures
to share**

Acknowledgements

Our thanks to the many contributors who have allowed their poems or imagery to be used for a reduced or no fee.

Published by

Pictures to Share Community Interest Company.
Tattenhall, Cheshire

www.picturestoshare.co.uk

Graphics by Duncan Watts
Printed in Europe

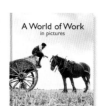

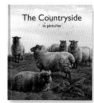

To see our other titles go to
www.picturestoshare.co.uk